Life on the Yorkshire P

Compiled by W. R. Mitchell

A SHIPPON IN NIDDERDALE

Dalesman Books
1984

TROTTING EVENT AT THE WENSLEYDALE SHOW

The Dalesman Publishing Company Ltd., Clapham, via Lancaster LA2 8EB
© Dalesman Publishing Company Ltd., 1984. ISBN: 0 85206 758 5
Printed in Great Britain by Fretwell & Brian Ltd.,
Healey Works, Goulbourne Street, Keighley, West Yorkshire

Contents

★   ★   ★

Our Cover Pictures: Front — Ken Wilde, the farmer whose land is crossed by the six lanes of the M62. (Photographed for a Yorkshire Television production). Back — A Donkey Derby at Scissett, near Denbydale.

Right: Hebden Bridge

An Introduction

THERE IS A FANCIFUL THEORY that the Pennines were raised to keep the folk of Yorkshire and Lancashire apart. Geographers tell of much more ancient processes. To a traveller in the days of the first Elizabeth, the Pennines were "mountains waste, solitary, unpleasant and unsightly." Today, their special wilderness quality is enjoyed by thousands of regular visitors. Some climb the gritstone faces, and others descend potholes or squeeze their way into caves. Among the walkers are those who set out from Derbyshire on a 250-mile journey into Scotland, following the Pennine Way, the second longest continuous footpath in Britain.

Defoe referred to the Pennines as a "wall of brass". In places, the wall is breached. I was reared at Skipton, in the Aire Gap, and this historic town — which became industrialised without losing its old character as a marketing centre — has the best of two worlds. It is virtually ringed by lonely moors, but you do not have to travel far to the north to encounter limestone. There is nothing like limestone for brightening up a landscape. Elsewhere, the gritstone obtrudes. The walker's feet sink into peat that has the colour and consistency of good chocolate cake. The legs of the walker are whipped by the stems of heather.

As a boy in Skipton I saw the farmers of Wharfedale and Malham Moor in town for the day, patronising an auction mart that has a thoroughly industrial setting, with Mr. Dewhurst's mill on one side and a busy railway station and goods yard on the other. Steam rose from the mill, and the vapour from innumerable steam locomotives clouded the air around the railway, which at one time transported the farm stock — gentle Shorthorns, hill sheep of several breeds. Calves, swathed in sacking, lay patiently on station platforms.

At the head of the High Street was the gateway to the Clifford castle, with the big drum towers and motto carved in stone, Des or Mais, meaning "Henceforward." Mr. Dewhurst built his enormous mill at the other end of town, and the red-brick chimney had the visual impact of an exclamation mark. The mill buzzer provided daily time checks for the population.

Nowhere, on the direct line between Edale and Kirk Yetholm, does the Pennine Way reach the 3,000 feet contour. By continental standards, the Pennines are modest in their height. The weather systems beat against a north-south barrier. The Pennine climate can be every bit as severe as that in the Scottish Highlands. One of England's highest recorded wind speeds, 134 miles an hour, was noted on Great Dun Fell in January, 1968. When a rain gauge was set up at Ribblehead in 1954, the first annual total was 109½ inches. Lightning struck one of the rain gauges at Malham Tarn House, 1,000 feet above sea level in Craven, in 1983. Snow, borne here by north-easterly winds, has drifted to clog the landscape to a depth of 15 feet.

There has been human life on the Pennines for some 8,000 years. The first to arrive were hunting parties who summered on the fellsides and fished in the glacial lakes. Celtic folk named the rivers Wharfe and Nidd, and also Penyghent, one of the Three Peaks of Craven. Penyghent stands in an area where Norse names are the language of topography. When Angles and Danes had settled in the main valleys, the Norsemen arrived from the west, establishing a pattern of pastoral life that is still recognisably Norse. Among the Norse names are *fell, beck, hill, tarn, moss, heath and ling.*

The Pennines appear to be a wilderness, until you notice evidence of human activity, and realise that wherever you walk someone has been there before you. For centuries, packhorses provided a service between settlements, following the green ways, crossing streams by means of high-arched bridges. The trade declined with the transport revolution of last century. Manufacturers in the West Riding sent out wool to be spun in villages and at farms over a wide area, until man's inventiveness produced machines capable of doing at great speed what had previously been work for nimble fingers.

The Pennines were undoubtedly a barrier, and early travellers set foot on them with trepidation. They were not considered beautiful. Housman referred to "those

Left: Leeds and Liverpool Canal at Saltaire.

numerous and extensive bleak moors which present themselves on all hands to the eye of the traveller." When the woolmen of the West Riding lifted their eyes to the Pennine Hills, they were not seeking a religious experience. From the hills came good building stone, and delightfully soft water — ideal for many industrial processes — and also sheep, yielding wool for processing.

The Bronte sisters, writing at their draughty parsonage just south of the Aire Gap, made the moorland environment their own. It is in the Bronte Country that the outcropping stone seems especially dark, but in summer the scene is relieved by the acres of cotton grass (it is really a sedge), which whitens many a plateau as though with snow. The gleaming plant can be seen from some of the high roads leading from Haworth, including that to Stanbury and on to Lancashire, and another running from Oxenhope to Hebden Bridge.

Living on or around the Pennines is a special type of person — one who is not discomfited by long winters and climatic excesses, who has a jaunty spirit and an appetite for work. J. B. Priestley, writing about dalesfolk, mentioned some Dales farmers who were like minor characters from Ibsen. The farmers, like the sheep they tend, are "heafed"; they have formed a strong allegiance to the birthplaces, to the spots where they drank their mothers' milk.

The mill-workers of old formed a select community, bound together through concern for the mill and regard for the little chapels at which most of their Sundays were spent. Work lasted for six and a-half days. John Hartley observed:

At hauf past five Tha leaves thi bed,
And off Tha goes to wark;
An gropes thi way to Mill or Shed,
Six months o' th'year in th'dark.
Tha gets but little for Thi pains,
But that's no fault o' Thine,
Thi Master reckons up his gains,
An ligs in bed till nine.

The Pennine folk were able to offset, against the grim hours of toil, the joy of chapel "do's", of concerts, pie suppers, whist drives and music-making. Brass bands flourished in the industrial towns that back on to the Pennines. Some names of bands are world-famous. Who has not heard of the Brighouse & Rastrick and Black Dyke Mills?

In the soot-blackened streets of Calderdale, at Easter, the pace-egging play is still enacted. St. George slays the dragon — and, ritualistically, there is the triumph of good over evil. Pennine folk who were keen to laugh often did so at the expense of their neighbours, such as the Slaithwaite (Slawit) Moonrakers of the Colne Valley. They were said to have seen the moon's reflection in the canal. Believing it to be a cheese, they attempted to get it out with a rake! At Marsden, local men tried to wall in a cuckoo, in the hope of retaining the good weather which invariably departed when the bird flew off to its wintering grounds. Cricket was played on grounds (not always level) in the shadow of the mills. Some folk played "poor man's golf", alias knur and spell. The knur was a ball, which was placed on a spell and struck by a stick.

The jauntiness of West Riding life — and the beauty of the moorland setting for one of the towns, Holmfirth — have been enjoyed by a large television audience for the series Last of the Summer Wine, in which three men seek to occupy their time interestingly now that they are no longer able to work. In the short Pennine summer, the moors are the "lungs" of the urban communities. They are so easily attained. At Todmorden, two terms are used — "uplands" for the grassy parts and "moors" for the heathery ridges. You can stand on some of these high places, only a mile or so from town, without being aware of the concentration of buildings — the mills, terraced houses, shops, old pubs, railway viaducts, weed-fringed canal. They are tucked out of sight in a fold of the landscape. You look, instead, across the high ground, where the ridges are like waves in a petrified sea, and the only really prominent features are memorials like that on Stoodley Pike. Everyone knows Haworth, which clings to a hillside; more and more people are discovering Heptonstall, which is a hilltop village, its old houses set on a ledge overlooking miles of the Southern Pennines.

The late Phyllis Bentley, who wrote extensively about the Southern Pennines, once told a newspaper interviewer of the thing that specially appealed to her. "When I was a little girl, the two things I knew most about were hills and mills . . . I was always very proud of living in the West Riding of Yorkshire, in that hilly part which is called the backbone of England, the Pennine Chain . . . At night I loved to see the lighted trams climbing up the dark hills like fireflies on black velvet; it seemed to me that they were brave and sturdy, like Yorkshire people, not afraid of difficult tasks or big hills."

The West Riding exists only in memory. It has been hacked about to suit the bureaucratic process. Dentdale was handed to Cumbria, and much of Bowland to Lancashire. Large new local government units were created where once there was a collection of proud and fiercely independent towns. The photographs on these pages, submitted to *The Dalesman* over the years, celebrate the spirit of Pennine folk and record some of their activities . . .

Acknowledgements . . .

Calder News Agency: 52 (left), 57. *Ken Dawson:* 55 (bottom right). *Collection of Ian Dewhirst:* 38 (right). *John Edenbrow:* 23, 31 (right). *Norman Evans:* 24 (left). *J. R. Fawcett:* 12 (right). *Fellsman Hike:* 27 (right). *John Forder:* 16 (top left), 26. *GPO:* 19 (bottom left). *George W. Hare:* 18. *Cyril Harrington:* 62 (bottom right). *J. L. Hepworth:* 48. *R. and L. Hinson:* 17. *Gordon R. Hopkins:* 42, 43. *Ledbetter:* Title Page, 63. *Denis P. McCarthy:* 52 (right), 53.

Edwin Mitchell: 38 (left). *W. R. Mitchell:* 11, 12 (left), 16 (bottom left), 16 (right), 19 (top left), 19 (right), 21, 55 (top right). *John S. Murray:* 15, 20 (right). *Alan Parker:* 27 (top left). *Tom Parker:* 24 (right), 28 (left), 31 (bottom left), 62 (left). *Enid M. Pyrah:* 34 (left), 37. *H. W. Rhodes:* 9. *Robert Rixon:* 20 (bottom left). *Clifford Robinson:* 3, 10, 13, 28 (right), 29, 30, 32, 34 (top right), 39, 40, 41, 44, 45, 46, 47, 50, 51, 54, 55 (left), 58, 59. *Bertram Unne:* 7, 20 (top left). *Derek Widdicombe:* Back Cover, 14, 33, 35, 60. *Christine Whitehead:* 25, 36. *Rex Williams:* 4. *J. Winterburn:* 31 (top left). *Geoffrey N. Wright:* 2. *Yorkshire Television:* Front Cover.

TAKING SHEEP BACK TO THE MOOR NEAR GAYLE, WENSLEYDALE

Alan Spence (Bingley Harriers) descending Ingleborough in the 1973 Three Peaks Race. He was placed fifth with a time of 2hr. 45min. 08sec.

The Northern Fells

YORKSHIRE extended as far north as Mickle Fell. It stretched a finger of land to tickle the ribs of Westmorland. Yorkshire also extended to the Tees. The reorganisation of the county boundaries in 1974 meant that much ground was handed over to Cumbria. Not only was Mickle Fell lost, but the second highest peak — Whernside, at 2,419 feet — was to be shared, in the sense that the county boundary runs across the summit. We must now fall back on Ingleborough (2,363 feet) . . .

This is not so much a peak as a collection of fells. There is elation in exploring them. The "attic" is a windswept plateau, vantage point for some long views across the Pennines, to Lakeland and across to the western sea. Having a substantial layer of limestone, Ingleborough has extensive "cellars". Pictured on the right is one of the big open shafts, Alum Pot, the potholer looking towards the surface from a point about 100 feet below the surface.

The land on and around the Three Peaks has a high scenic value. Here is classic limestone country. The peaks are "capped" by millstone grit, which is impervious to water. The streams flow down the Yoredale Series of rocks — alternating bands of shales, grits and limestone — and disappear down cracks in the limestone. Potholers joyfully follow their underground courses.

The Three Peaks foot race (in spring) and cyclo-cross (in autumn) have courses of about 25 miles, with some 5,000 feet of climbing. Entrants complete the course in considerably less than three hours!

SUNBEAMS IN ALUM POT

For years, Tan Hill Inn — England's highest licensed premises, at 1,732 feet — were in Yorkshire. The boundary change means that they are in County Durham, but "nobbut just". It's an area where the Swaledale breed of sheep is seen at its best, the breed having evolved from a type fixed by farmers living on and around Tan Hill. Some sheep beg food from the motorists!

A farmer pictured at Darnbrook some 20 years ago. Pennine farming is largely influenced by the duration and severity of the winter. Cattle are in-wintered; the sheep must be provided with hay in the worst periods. This man was wearing clogs, a type of footwear that lifts the feet well above the ground and has a reputation for "turning snow broth."

A Pennine roadman, photographed between Malham Tarn and Darnbrook, was well protected from the rain. The road is a much-used route between Cowside (near Langcliffe) and Cowside (near Arncliffe).

On Market Day

THERE IS MUCH MORE to a Dales market than buying and selling. It is also an event at which reunions take place between old friends. Gossip, which has been described as "the small change of rural life", is — exchanged. Sedbergh **(pictured left)** is now in Cumbria, but for centuries this was a far northern outpost of Yorkshire. The market stalls have an especially attractive setting, near the old church.

Pictured above are early shoppers in the street at Richmond by the Swale. The photograph was taken about 30 years ago. The modern photograph **(right)** is of the Friday market at Leyburn, in Wensleydale. The range of commodities for sale is breath-taking; the area covered immense. Next morning, the market place returns to its more normal role of providing parking space for cars.

A modern sport in a Dales setting. Water skiers prepare their boats and equipment at Semerwater, near Bainbridge, in Wensleydale. When the boating season is over, the lake is quiet again — and a herd of whooper swans flies in, using it as a winter sanctuary.

The moors near Bolton Abbey, in Wharfedale, are among the best known in Britain. When the grouse-shooting season begins in August, there are Royal guests in the party. The photograph shows beaters dispersing prior to a "drive".

The domino-players at Dent were born in Yorkshire and became Cumbrians with the local government reorganisation in 1974. The game, and the quality of the ale, remains the same! Middleham, in Wensleydale **(left)** is noted for its racing stables. The horses are exercised on the local moors. Dipping sheep **(above)** is a comparatively modern activity, here being practised near Settle. At one time sheep were covered with salve each November to discourage insect pests.

Dalesfolk

THE OLDEST of the dalesfolk living today remember times of great austerity, when thrift was a necessity. In those days the families living at the farms and cottages of the upper dales were virtually independent of the outside world. They grew much of what they ate. There were craftsmen in every district — blacksmith, joiner, wheelwright, mason — to do the special tasks. Nothing was wasted. The Swaledale farmer **(pictured right)** was collecting the stalks of heather, blackened and charred after a tract of moor had been fired. The stalks would be used for kindling.

It was a continuously hard life, all bed and work. Some of the kindling was placed beneath the "copper" in which water was heated for the weekly wash. The kitchen fire was fuelled by "cowlings", as the heather stalks were known; by wood, peat and Tan Hill coal. The coal, removed from the measures in the Yoredale Series of rocks, tended to be hard but once ignited developed a relentless heat.

Tending the cattle and sheep were the major tasks on the farms. The dalesfolk kept Shorthorn cattle, and in the upper dales it was not unknown for the animals to be milked out of doors in summer, the stool being "stored" on a walltop. The cows queued up and were provided with a measure of food to keep them calm and happy. When the warble fly was active, and the cows were "gadding", the milkmaid — and this type of milking was usually a task for a girl or young woman — had a frustrating time keeping the cattle still.

There were endless tasks with sheep, which were to be gathered on the fells for lambing, dipping, spaining (separation of ewes and lambs), also for clipping, once performed with hand-shears, the clippers sitting on special wooden "stools". It was not unknown for neighbours to come together to clip. Afterwards they enjoyed a substantial meal and — if there was any remaining energy — a dance to music provided by fiddle and melodeon.

The old sense of isolation is unknown today, when there is quick, convenient transport on good roads, and every house is linked to the world by radio or television. Many of the craftsmen had to close the doors of their workshops when goods and services became handily available from dealers in the market towns.

Bolton Castle, the historic fortified house of the Scropes in Wensleydale, provides a dramatic backdrop to a meet of local riders. Today, the castle has a folk museum and a restaurant. From the castle, a visitor can look far across a broad valley which, extending from west to east, provides travellers with an easy crossing point of the Pennine range.

Top, left: The village shop at Austwick, as it was a quarter of a century ago. **Left:** Postman and postwoman leave on their rounds from the post office at Bolton Abbey, in Wharfedale. **Above:** Part of the winter round on a sheep farm is taking hay to the stock. In our picture is Gordon Falshaw, of Hubberholme.

Scenes in Wharfedale. **Top, left:** A bite before milking at Laund Farm, Bolton Abbey. **Left:** Lambing time at Kettlewell. **Above:** Spreading muck near Appletreewick. **Right:** In the limestone country. A shepherd near Langcliffe, North Ribblesdale.

Limestone Country

BEAUTY is far more than skin deep in the Three Peaks country of North Craven, where the limestone is honeycombed by potholes and caves — well over 1,000 systems, descending with enormous "pitches" to the impervious slate. They were created by rainwater which picked up a weak solution of acid from the atmosphere and vegetation, flowing underground through cracks and crannies, enlarging and adorning them with glistening formations.

This is a world which can be visited by the holidaymaker, as at Ingleborough Cave near Clapham and White Scar Cave near Ingleton. There are concrete paths, and electric lighting to reveal the way and illuminate some of the formations — the stalactites (which grow down from the roof through the steady dripping of water over many years) and stalagmites (formed from water dripping on to the floor). The two can combine to form a pillar.

Pictured on the left are potholers exploring Alum Pot, near Selside in North Ribblesdale, using the Long Churn approach to a system that reaches a depth of almost 300 feet. This is a system to be explored with experienced leaders. Putting a green dye in the water established that the water from Alum Pot flows *under* the Ribble, and emerges to flow into the river on the side opposite that from which it originated!

The Buckhaw Brow stretch of the A65, just north of Settle, is spectacular, with limestone crags on one side and gritstone terrain dipping on the other side. The road is on the line of a geological fault. Water from the limestone appears in the Ebbing and Flowing Well **(pictured right)**. The water level rises and falls from time to time. Some people believed its behaviour was controlled by the tides of Morecambe Bay! There may be a double syphon in the rock behind. Times of moderate rainfall appear to be the best times for observing a remarkable phenomenon.

Above: Thornton Force, in a deep glen near Ingleton. **Right**: An unusually large cairn on a remote shelf of limestone, Ingleborough. **Opposite page**: Driving Dalesbred sheep down the green lane — part of the Pennine Way — near Horton-in-Ribblesdale.

Hale and Hearty

Opposite page: The modern cave diver, photographed in Kingsdale. **This page, top left:** Cyclists on Mastiles Lane descend towards Wharfedale. **Left:** John Rawnsley, who organises the annual Three Peaks Cyclo-cross, negotiates some rough country. **Above:** Walkers on the annual Fellsman Hike arrive at the Kingsdale checkpoint.

Left: Climbing on the limestone wall of Malham Cove. **Above:** Gritstone climbing, at the Cow and Calf Rocks above Ilkley, in mid-Wharfedale. **Right:** Morris dancers entertain townsfolk and visitors in the Valley Gardens at Harrogate.

Horses — and some donkeys. **Opposite page:** The famous old packhorse bridge at Wycollar, which — though lying in Lancashire — is also part of "Bronteland". **Top, left:** Lime dressing in the Dales, an old photograph. **Left:** Donkeys near Hebden Bridge. **Above:** Shibden Valley, near Halifax.

On the "Cut"

OFFICIALLY, it is a canal; to many West Riding families it is the "cut". Going for a walk on "t'cut bank" was a diverting, and cheap, pastime. At the Five Rise Locks, Bingley **(pictured left)** the Leeds and Liverpool Canal reaches a peak of interest. The locks made it possible for boats to negotiate a rise of 60 feet, each lock making it possible for a boat to gain 12 feet. Where there are locks, there are gatherings of people in summer. The small boy **(right)** was at Apperley Bridge, near Bradford.

The Leeds and Liverpool Canal, linking two great industrial centres — and also providing a connection between the ports of Liverpool and Hull — is no longer of great consequence as a commercial enterprise. Its use by the owners of pleasure craft increases year by year. There are, inevitably, "honeypots" that draw the crowds. One of them is Skipton, where the Springs Canal provides a short spur once used for the transit of quarry material. Among the other points of concentration is East Marton, west of Skipton, where there are moorings near an unusual feature of the canal — a double-arched bridge, the lower bridge crossing the canal and the one above lifting the level to that of the road.

In this area, the beauty of the canal's setting is to be appreciated. It is a soft pastoral beauty. The canal was excavated between the rounded grassy hills that are drumlins, heaps of material left with the melting of glacial ice. Old churches look as though they have been forgotten for centuries (though are used regularly). Among them, standing in solitude not far from the canal, is St. Peter's church at Marton.

In contrast are the industrial areas. A walker by the canal, or one who is at the helm of a boat, sees the "back doors" of the towns, and especially of the mills. There was an old man at Skipton called Billy Gelling who made his

living gathering coal from the bed of the canal behind Dewhurst's mill. Any coal spilled was left for him. He operated with a bucket-like container, in which holes had been made, attached to a long pole. It was known for kindly bargees to actually drop some coal over the side for the benefit of Billy!

Between Leeds and Liverpool. **Left and above**: At Banknewton, near Gargrave. **Right**: Between Bradley and Kildwick. **Opposite page**: On the Broughton side of Skipton.

Above: The Leeds and Liverpool Canal at East Marton, near Skipton. **Opposite page:** "Time for lunch" — a quiet moment by the canal at Skipton.

Valley of the Worth

Left: Laying the North Sea gas pipeline towards Keighley. The photograph was taken on the edge of Addingham High Moor. **Above**: Keighley's new shopping centre. **Below**: How the 1918 Victory was celebrated at Keighley. **Opposite page**: Steam locomotive on Worth Valley Line, and a modern bus at Haworth.

Opposite page: The Thrill of Steam. Children watching locomotives on the Worth Valley Line, which connects Keighley with Haworth. **Above:** Steam-up on the Worth Valley — a photograph taken at Haworth station. The Railway was a local enterprise until 1881, and then the Midland Railway Company took it over. Passenger services were withdrawn at the end of 1961, but happily a preservation society was formed. Steam continues to be used on the system.

Walking at Whitsuntide

Photographs from the village of East Morton, near Keighley, where the Walk was revived in 1982 and the band played in a spirited way to keep the feet moving. The terrace of houses **(left)** is Providence Row. Tea was served in the Institute and the revival was pronounced to be "a reight good do".

The Calderdale Pace-eggers

On Good Friday, the Pace Egg players are active in the towns and villages of the Calder Valley. The photographs on these pages were taken at Hebden Bridge. First comes Ringer-In or Bold Slasher, followed by St. George, the Doctor, the Black Prince of Paradise and Owd Tosspot. The first two and the Black Prince carry swords and wear helmets and tunics festooned with ribbons. The Doctor is complete with top-hat, morning coat and small black bag. Tosspot has donned a motley collection of rags: he carries a basket and his Owd Betty, a scarecrow-like female doll. The Pace Egg is a relation of the Mummer's Plays of other parts of England and is distantly related to the old Miracle Plays. The Heptonstall Version is used today.

Fred Raine setting up his loom for weaving in the Colne Valley Craft Museum at Golcar, near Huddersfield.

The futuristic layout of a new shopping centre at Bradford — a city that was once famous for its Victorian edifices.

The Sporting Life. **Opposite page:** These photographs were taken at Hunslet in 1954 when a 500 year old game was revived by Eddie Thompson and Mr. Robinson of the "Old Engine Hotel". Knur and spell was once popular throughout the North. Some of the tackle used is preserved in museums, including Bankfield at Halifax. In 1899, a knur and spell player called Joe Machin, who lived near Barnsley, hit a pot knur weighing half an ounce for a distance of just over 15 score yards.
Above: Enthusiasts in the early days of motor cycling challenged old tracks on the Pennines. In this photograph, taken by the late C. H. Wood, Mr. J. Marshall rests at the roadside while his smoking 1912 P and M cools off after the long climb from Ilkley to Keighley Gate.

Left: Among the features of the Southern Pennines are the steep, winding roads, characterised by stone setts. This stretch is between Boulder Clough and Mytholmroyd. **Above**: Shipley Glen has long been a favourite leisure time haunt of families living in the Aire Valley. One attraction is the rack railway; other visitors are content to walk in a moorland setting.

Two Pennine Wallers

Below: John Leslie Haworth. **Opposite page**: Tom Chapman. They are at work on the moors above Todmorden.

Harvesting dock leaves by the river at Hebden Bridge. The leaves were needed for making dock pudding, those used being leaves of the "sweet dock", which is different from the common dock. Leaves are boiled, along with onions, oatmeal and seasoning, to make a pudding that is still popular in the area.

Springtime on the Southern Pennines

A view near Holmfirth; the dark gritstone is offset by the golden heads of daffodils.

Above: Old Bradford, complete with soot. The city has been transformed with a rebuilding programme and brisk cleaning of the remaining Victorian buildings. **Below:** Preservation on an imposing scale — the Piece Hall at Halifax, viewed from one of the balconies.

Above: Walkers take a break for refreshment at Luddenden, the view including a 17th century inn that was known to Branwell Bronte.

A Place for Craftsmanship

Left: At the Craft Museum at Golcar. **Above:** Attending to clog soles at Hebden Bridge.

Eric Clayton examining shuttles in Fearnside's picturesque workshop, in the Calder Valley.

"Summer Wine" Country

COMPO, Foggy and Clegg, of the television series "Last of the Summer Wine", have given to Holmfirth a special fame. We all like to laugh, and the antics of the trio, in recognisably Holmfirth settings, has provided many a face massage as we responded to the pithy Yorkshire humour. Visitors to Holmfirth seek out the famous steps leading to "Norah Batty's" house **(opposite page, right)**.

A guide book referred to Holmfirth as "a small grey town busy with wool"; it occupies a deep valley. The builders of the houses did their best to cope with ground on the slant. The buildings were fashioned of native stone, splendidly dressed, as at the church **(left)** and houses around the Square **(opposite page, top left)**. Local buildings were blackened by the long years of industrial pollution. The Square itself shows further evidence of the stonemason's skill in the substantial flags, on some of which are displayed goods from a local hardware store. In the corner of this picture is the building used as a cafe in the television production of "Last of the Summer Wine". Holmfirth is also rich in passage ways and steps.

Those who have watched the television programme will be aware of extensive moors above the narrow valley. I recall visiting Holme Moss on the day television came to the North. There, 1,725 feet above sea level, on a widespreading tract of moorland, I watched as the television transmitter station was officially opened. The mast I saw rose for 750 feet, being braced by cables, which from a distance seemed as insubstantial as spider webs. The tapered base of the huge mast rested on a large ball bearing, permitting the mast slight movement in any direction, for winds with speeds up to 125 miles an hour have been recorded on these "tops".

"Summer Wine" Country has many fast-flowing becks and reservoirs. The river Holme, which makes a rapid descent, has periodically flooded. The flood of 1738 lapped into the church as local people were at their prayers. There was a great flood in 1777, and in 1852, when Bilberry Reservoir burst. Then an estimated 90 million gallons of water swept through the valley causing the deaths of 81 people and resulting in considerable damage to property.

Above: Products of the good earth. The Harvest Festival decorations on the altar of St. Lawrence's Church, Pudsey. **Opposite page:** Restoring a canal. The Huddersfield Canal Society's trip-boat "Stan" in front of Tunnel End Cottages. This organisation has done much to restore an ancient form of Pennine transport.

A Pennine Snowtime

Above: Thornton Force, near Ingleton, frozen as a slab of ice 50 feet high and up to five feet in thickness.

Above: Winter lays hold of an Airedale Farm. **Below:** A timber wagon at the top of Buckhaw Brow, near Settle. **Opposite page:** Funeral by horse-drawn sleigh on the moors between Otley and Horsforth in the grim winter of 1947.

Bobus and Butterley Reservoir from Binn Moor, on the Pennine Way near Marsden, Yorkshire. The area is part of the Peak District National Park.